George N. Nissenson

Practical Treatise on Injectors

As Feeders of Steam Boilers

George N. Nissenson

Practical Treatise on Injectors
As Feeders of Steam Boilers

ISBN/EAN: 9783743465107

Manufactured in Europe, USA, Canada, Australia, Japa

Cover: Foto ©Lupo / pixelio.de

Manufactured and distributed by brebook publishing software
(www.brebook.com)

George N. Nissenson

Practical Treatise on Injectors

PRACTICAL TREATISE

—on—

INJECTORS

As Feeders of Steam Boilers,

FOR THE USE OF

MASTER MECHANICS AND ENGINEERS IN CHARGE OF
LOCOMOTIVE, MARINE AND STATIONARY BOILERS.

With Numerous Cuts.

BY

GEORGE N. NISSENSON,

Engineer.

NEW YORK:
1890.
PUBLISHED BY THE AUTHOR.

PREFACE.

ALTHOUGH the above title expresses, as I believe, with sufficient explicitness the scope and the purpose of this volume, yet I find it desirable to say a few words for the better understanding of it, in order to prevent the possibility of any disappointment on the part of those who may be looking for such information in this book, which they will be apt not to find in it. There being no separate work on Injectors, which could be consulted with advantage by those who are using this apparatus daily, and having keenly felt the want of it as a practical man myself, I came to think, that I might render a service to the profession of Engineers and Mechanics by publishing such a one. As a matter of course, I confine myself in it strictly to what is of importance and practical value to those who are operating Injectors, but not to those who are manufacturing them. In consequence of this, the theory of the apparatus and its principles will be gone into only so far as they are apt to facilitate the practice, and can be made comprehensive enough, even to that man who hardly has any opportunity for theoretical studies. The main object of the book is to enlighten the great army of practical Engineers as to How an Injector Works, and if it fails to perform its duties satisfactorily, to show where to look for the cause, so as to be able TO MAKE IT WORK.

Besides the general principles which are common to all Injectors, the reader will find in this volume the description and the direction for operating all the most approved patterns of Injectors now in use, together with the details of their respective improvements.

Should this effort of mine meet the approval of those for whom this book is published, I propose to issue similar practical treatises on various mechanical appliances, apparatuses, and machines, about which reliable information cannot be easily obtained, causing thereby considerable inconvenience to the practical men, who have neither the time nor the opportunity to hunt it up for themselves in the professional Reports and in the periodical publications.

THE AUTHOR.

160 East 109th Street,
New York City, August, 1890.

CONTENTS.

INTRODUCTION.

INJECTOR, which is now rapidly superseding all other appliances for feeding steam boilers, was, as is always the case with the products of man's ingenuity and industry, defective in many respects when it came out of the hand of the first inventor. However, this must not detract an iota from the merits of that man and diminish the service he has rendered to industry, much more so as the principle upon which this mechanical contrivance is based proved itself to be applicable to various other useful purposes. Every injector, in the first place, is necessarily an ejector, for the same reason that every feed pump is at the same time a draw out or exhaust pump, because in pumping into one receiver it must pump out its stuff from some other one. The special object in view, it is true, modifies in each case the construction of the apparatus, but the principle remains one and the same.

Although Giffard, the inventor, has designed his injector for feeding steam boilers, yet the principle which he had so ingeniously utilized was since applied to numerous other purposes. Interesting as it would most likely be for the reader to become acquainted with the various applications of this principle and the gradual development of the apparatus it is based upon, we find it necessary to abstain from going into these details, as, in the first place, it would take much more space than we have at our command, and in the second, because it would be a deviation from our programme.

The knowledge of various methods and means employed

by different inventors for the sake of increasing the efficiency of the apparatus can be of practical value only to manufacturers or other inventors, but not to that class of persons whom we have exclusively in view. However, a short historical notice will not be out of place here.

The action of a fluid or gas issuing from an orifice with great velocity, and carrying along with it some other fluid or semi-fluid with which it comes in contact on its route, was known in 1570. And there are reasons for supposing that it was understood much earlier, because every man in expectorating or forcing a strong current of air through the cavity of his nose, for the purpose of getting rid of the secretion which has aecumulated inside of his nostrils, utilizes this principle of injector and uses it as an ejector. Stephenson took advantage of this phenomenon and applied it in 1820 as the well-known blast pipe on locomotives. Gurney's steam ventilator acted by means of steam passing through one pipe and sucking air through another connected with it. This simple apparatus was afterwards employed by Nagel and Kaemp in centrifugal pumps to prevent filling. Besides these may be mentioned Thompson's pump, the water bellows, and Danchell's manometer.

But it was reserved for Giffard in 1853 to utilize it for feeding steam boilers, and the advantages of this method over the old ones were so numerous and apparent, that it was speedily recognized and introduced everywhere when steam was used as a motive power.

In this country it was introduced by Messrs. Wm. Sellers & Co. of Philadelphia in 1860, with very important improvements. In Europe Giffard's injector underwent a series of very important modifications in the hands of Del-Peche, Kraus, Korting, Friedmann, and others. The improvements consist mainly in the more judicious arrangement of parts of the apparatus, and in replacing others by new attachments, which increase the effectiveness and facilitate its operation. Amongst the American recent inventions may be mentioned the Hancock's, Rue's, Desmond's, Penberthy's, Murdock's, and Eberman's, which will be fully described at the proper place.

The injector, as it is now manufactured, must be looked upon as being a very satisfactory apparatus, and it has been proved by a number of practical tests, that for relative economy of steam and for constant duty, it is the most efficient for feeding steam boilers, and is destined to supersede all other methods of feed. This is getting to be generally understood and properly appreciated by intelligent engineers, much more so because from experience they had learned that it requires less attention on the part of the operator, as the best injectors are self-adjusting and fulfill their requirements under all conditions of duty, being at the same time less liable to get out of order, and not requiring consequently so frequent and so expensive repairs, as the ordinary pump does.

In using the injector no difficulty is experienced in adjusting the openings for steam and water, so as to produce a constant and regular supply of any required quantity of water to the boiler without waste from the overflow, while the feed, at the same time, may be varied sufficiently to meet the varying demand.

When considering the performance of the injector as compared with that of the steam pump, we arrive at the result that an injector, heat not considered, consumes a little more steam than the steam pump of equal performance. But with regard to the heat which steam communicates to the feed water the result is by no means so unfavorable. The heat expended in warming the water amounts to eighty-one per cent., that converted into work to nineteen per cent.; so that there is no direct loss of heat. However, a more advantageous method of heating the feed water can be obtained by sending the delivery water through an exhaust heater. The steam employed in working the injector is returned to the boiler with the feed water, raising thereby its temperature, and preventing the unequal expansion, so disastrous to boiler plates caused by pumping in water at a low temperature. The importance of an independent feed on locomotive engines by means of an injector should be evident to everyone who is familiar with running locomotives. Up to the time of the introduction of Giffard's injector, donkey pumps or plunger pumps, driven by either eccentric or cross-head, were the usual methods of feed, and the latter are still in service on many of the old pattern. But since the invention of the injector it has gradually driven out of use the contrivances just mentioned, and nearly all of the new engines built during the last two years have two injectors attached, one on each side of the boiler.

That for locomotive engines the injector is the most reliable and efficient instrument which can be used with advantage, has been proved by a series of experiments conducted by a committee appointed at the convention of the Master Mechanics' Association in 1875. The experiments have been made with a No. 6 Friedmann injector, attached to a freight engine of the Illinois Central Railroad Company. The result of the experiments did show that the engine burned 9.08 per cent. more coal and used 4.4 per cent. more water while running with the pump. Other experiments were also made to determine the temperature of water injected into the boiler, as well as the quantity of water which a No. 6 Friedmann injector would force into the boiler in a given length of time. The committee, in presenting the results, states that the injector is as reliable as a pump, and produces a small saving in fuel; at the same time that the pressure is steadier and the boiler is subjected to fewer changes in temperature. The action of a pump connected to a cross-head is not regular, and it fails exactly at the time when there is the greatest demand for it. When the greatest regularity of feed is necessary, the movement of the pump is so fast as to render its action uncertain, and it wastes a maximum power while it produces a minimum result. When connected to a cross-head the pump brings a diagonal strain and uneven wear upon the cross-head and piston rod, thus materially increasing friction and repairs; moreover, in cold weather a momentary stoppage in the flow of water frequently allows the pump time to freeze.

THE PRINCIPLE OF INJECTOR.

Simple as the working of a well-constructed and properly adjusted injector may appear, it is by no means the case as to its theory. The phenomena involved in its operation are mainly those of thermodynamics, a comparatively new science, and their complexity in so far has defied mathematical analysis, as it regards the establishment of a general formula or of a series of formulæ, which would embrace its *modus operandi* in its full details. It is only by disregarding or assuming that some of the variations entering in its factors are insignificant in comparison with others, that we may arrive at a comprehensive statement of the principles involved in the injector. Approximate as such a theory must necessarily be, it is still better than none; besides, as it does not omit any of the main facts involved, but only the secondary ones, it gives tolerably true results, applicable to all cases as far as the main points are therein involved.

Moreover, accumulated experiences furnish us with additional data, which enable us to supplement the theory in all those cases where there happen to be any discrepancy or a failure on the part of the latter to give a satisfactory answer. In what follows we will present the theory in accordance with what we have just said, concentrating our attention on the main points, avoiding all complicating details, and endeavoring at the same time to be as comprehensive as the nature of the question will permit. In its principal feature the phenomenon, which the theory has to explain, consists in this.

A boiler containing live steam is tapped at the highest

point of the steam chamber, and a pipe bending down-
wards is inserted in the opening. To its open end is
attached an injector, communicating with the water chamber of the same boiler, and receiving at the same time a
supply of water at lower temperature from another source.
This last water is driven into the boiler by the steam of the
same boiler through the help of the injector.

The question arises, How can steam obtained from the
top of the boiler, where the pressure is less than that at
the bottom of it, force additional water supply to the boiler
against a greater pressure than that under which it issues
itself?

Whenever a fluid (whether liquid or gas), inclosed in a
space, i.e., confined in it by some sort of pressure and the
resistance of the material inclosing that space, is let out of
it through an opening or an orifice, it will flow out, and
the quantity discharged through the orifice per unit of time
will depend principally upon the following circumstances:

(1) The pressure acting upon it inside of the inclosed
space;

(2) The density or the heaviness of the fluid possessed
under that pressure;

(3) The pressure existing in the space into which it
flows;

(4) The size and the form of the orifice; and

(5) The friction it is subjected to, which depends chiefly
upon the nature of the fluid and upon the smoothness and
roughness of the surfaces it comes in contact with, while
flowing out.

Each of the above indicated circumstances not only
may be different for each separate case, but they may also
vary during the flowing itself, and in fact they generally
do, as nothing in the universe remains unchanged for a
moment of time. But we will disregard all those varia-

tions for the sake of simplifying our problem, and, moreover, leave out of consideration the friction and the shape
of the orifice, assuming it simply to be of a certain size or
to have so many units of surface. In this way we will
reduce our principal conditions of flow to two first ones;
namely, to the pressures (inside and outside) and to the
density of the flowing fluid, assuming that they remain
unchanged during the flowage.

Let us see now what will be the velocity of steam
issuing from a boiler under certain pressure through an
opening of a unit of surface, say one inch. If the pressure
in the boiler is, for instance, five atmospheres, and the
temperature under which a complete saturation under that
pressure takes place is equal to 307° Fahr. scale, the
weight of 12 cubic inches of steam is about .001149. As
the flow takes place not into a vacuum, but has the pressure of one atmosphere acting against it, the effective head,
i.e., the head to which the flow is due, will be $5 — 1 = 4$
atmospheres, or as the pressure of one atmosphere on
a square inch amounts to 15 lbs., the total effective pressure
equals 4 times 15 lbs., or 60 lbs. Now, if we had a pipe,
with one inch sectional area, and wanted to fill it with the
steam at the above given temperature, so as to put into
that pipe the 60 lbs. of it, how long must that pipe be?
This length can be easily obtained by dividing the whole
weight representing the 4 atmospheric pressures or 60 lbs.
into the weight of 12 cubic inches of steam or .001149,
and will be 52,218. feet.

Now, if in accordance with the well known formula
$v = 8.008 \sqrt{h}$, where v stands for velocity; 8.008 is the
$\sqrt{64.4}$ or $\sqrt{2g}$, the acceleration of gravity, and h. is the
height or the length of our pipe; if we extract the square
root of the length and multiply it by 8.008, we will obtain
the velocity with which steam under the pressure of 4

atmospheres, and the temperature of 307° Fah., will flow
from an orifice of one square inch section, and which will
be $= 1834.7$ feet per second.

Let us now make one inch square opening at the bottom of the same boiler and see what will be the velocity of
the flow under the same effective head of 4 atmospheres.
As the excess of the pressure at the bottom of the boiler
due to the height of some 4 or 5 feet of water is small in
comparison with the 4 atmospheres, we will disregard it.
Performing the same operations as before, with the difference that instead of the weight of 12 cubic inches of steam
we must use the weight of 12 cubic inches of water, we will
have : $v = 8.008 \sqrt{136} = 92.96$ feet per second. Where
136 is the length of the pipe in feet, containing water corresponding to 4 atmospheric pressures, and is obtained by
dividing 60 lbs. into the weight of 12 cubic inches of water
$= .44.$

In comparing the velocity of steam, issuing from an inch
orifice under an effective pressure of 4 atmospheres, with
that of water under the same conditions, we see that the
former being 1834.7 ft. per second is about 20 times as
great as the latter, which is $=92.96$ feet per second.
Notwithstanding this large excess of velocity of steam over
that of water, it could not be made to enter the boiler for
this reason, that the momenta of these two opposing
streams are equal, as being due to the same force or pressure. The momentum, namely, is the product of the mass
by the velocity, and is expressed thus : $\frac{W}{g} v =$ momentum,
where $\frac{W}{g}$ is the weight w, divided into the acceleration of
gravity, g, which is equal to 32.2 ft. per second. And a
given force imparts velocities to two different bodies in-
versely proportional to their mass, or, what amounts to the
same, to their weights, or respective heaviness or densities.
But, by inserting an Injector we increase the momentum

on the steam side, and make it feed the boiler, by condensing the steam jet and mixing it with about 13 times more
water.   In its simplest form the apparatus is represented
on Fig. 1 in section.

When steam is admitted into the pipe A, through the

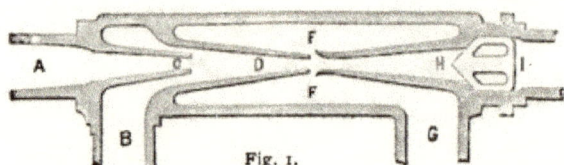

Fig. 1.

nozzle C, and, while escaping at a high velocity, is joined
by water, which flows in through the pipe B, and passes
around the nozzle G, thus condensing the steam in the
conical pipe D, it mingles with it and drives it through the
pipe H, into the boiler.

At an effective pressure of 60 lbs. per square inch, the
excess of velocity of the steam, as we know, is about in
the proportion of 20 to 1.   As the escaping steam in being
condensed loses none of its velocity, except that due to the
friction of the pipes through which it passes, consequently,
after condensation and mixing with 13 times more water,
it has yet a penetrating force sufficient to overcome the re-
sisting force of the water in the boiler.   At the moment of
condensation it imparts its momentum to the water by
which it is condensed, and with which it mingles.

Although the water coming through the pipe B has some
velocity, yet it may be left out of consideration as small in
comparison with that of steam.   Calling m the mass of
steam flowing out of the nozzle C in a unit of time, M
the mass of water which joins to it, v the velocity of
steam issuing from the nozzle C, V the velocity of the
liquefied steam mixed with water, which has just condensed
it, we must have, in order to obtain a complete liquefac-

tion of steam and produce an uninterrupted stream of water, the equality of momenta, i. e., $(m+M) \ V = m \ v$, wherefrom $V = \dfrac{m \ v}{m+M}$.

Now, if it is necessary that the liquid or the delivery jet should have 140° temperature, and that the temperature of admitted water has 59°, there must exist such a relation between the quantities of water and steam:[*]

$$59 \ M + 1202 \ m = 140 \ (m+M)$$
$$81 \ M = 1062 \ m$$
$$\frac{M}{m} = \frac{1062}{81} = 13.11$$

That is to say, there must be admitted 13 times more water than the steam weighs, in order to satisfy the above conditions and to obtain a complete liquefaction of steam, together with an unbroken stream for the feed.

Putting this value of M into the expression, $V = \dfrac{m \ v}{m+M}$, we will see that the velocity of mixture $= \frac{1}{14}$ of the initial velocity of steam, or dividing 1834.7 into 14, the velocity of the feed water $= 131$ feet per second, while, according to our calculation, the velocity of water issuing from the boiler was 92.96. The difference, $131 - 92.96, = 38.04$ feet, is amply sufficient to overcome all resistances and keep up a steady feed.

The above exposition shows how all such problems must be treated. When the circumstances are different, it is necessary only to substitute the data of the case in order to obtain the desired answer.

---

[*] In being condensed into water steam loses 990° Fah. units of heat, and adding 212° for the boiling point, its temperature is equal to ~~1062°~~. 1202°.

THE ACTION OF THE INJECTOR.

In considering the action of the injector regard must be had to four nozzles: the STEAM NOZZLE, through which the jet of steam is forced; the COMBINING NOZZLE, where the steam and water combine; the CONDENSING NOZZLE, in which condensation takes place, and which produces the vacuum; and the DELIVERY NOZZLE, through which the stream of water is driven into the boiler.

As soon as steam is admitted into the steam pipe it passes out through the steam nozzle, c, fig. 2, which is surrounded by the feed water that enters through the

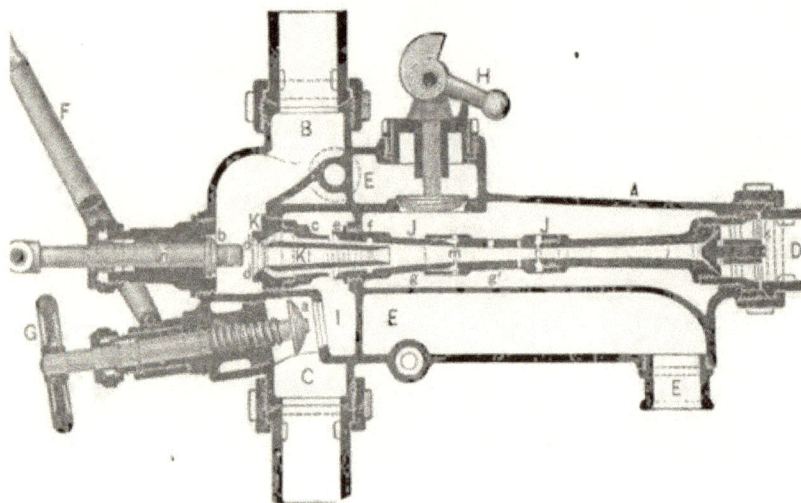

Fig. 2.

supply pipe into the combining nozzle, e, and with which it combines, being gradually reduced in volume and velocity until it reaches the condensing nozzle, n, where it is entirely converted into water, and **wherefrom** it **is** driven through the delivery nozzle, j, into the boiler, **while** it still possesses a momentum sufficient to lift up the check valve, to overcome the friction of the pipe and its bends, **and** to displace the water in the boiler ahead of **it**.

THE NOZZLES.

The certainty of action of an injector depends very much upon the construction of the nozzles and their dimensions, and that injector is the most advantageous which gives the greatest performance with the least consumption of steam.

The size of the bores of the nozzles are usually determined by the steam pressure to be employed and the quantity of water to be forced into a boiler.

Steam Nozzle.—The steam nozzle is a tube bored out straight in the middle and slightly conical towards its ends, reducing thereby the friction of the passing steam to its minimum. The bore of the steam nozzle at the straight point is varying, according to the quantity and velocity of steam desirable to attain.

Combining Nozzle.—The combining nozzle is generally bored out large at the entrance and tapered to allow the necessary quantity of water to pass around the annular space left between it and the steam nozzle. The former is so set inside of the condensing nozzle that its narrowest place comes exactly in the direction of the steam jet.

Condensing Nozzle.—The condensing nozzle forms the vacuum upon which depends the velocity of the supply water. With constant steam pressure and temperature of water the vacuum obtained is lower when the condensing nozzle is fed with too much or too little water. In the first case, because the jet of steam has not sufficient power to impel the water which gives a back pressure ; in the second case, because the temperature of the mixture is not low enough to condense the whole steam, and, consequently, the vacuum is lessened.

DELIVERY NOZZLE.—The delivery nozzle has the smallest bore of all the preceding nozzles, and upon it depends the volume of water to be forced into the boiler.

The numerical size of any injector is the diameter of the smallest part of the delivery nozzle expressed in milli-metres. Thus a No. 3 injector has an opening of 3 milli-metres in diameter, while a No. 9 injector measures 9 millimetres. The nozzles are made of a special metal, extra hard, in order to withstand the velocity of the flow and resist the wear, caused by impurities contained in water.

LIFTING INJECTOR.

In regard to the manner they get their water supply injectors are of two kinds: *lifting* and *non-lifting*. The former are generally placed above the level of the supply source, as for instance, in case of rivers, ponds or wells, where there is no available head, and they must raise their water, frequently up to 25 feet, before they drive it into the boiler.

The lifting of the water is effected by an independent jet of steam, escaping into the atmosphere through a lifting nozzle. Steam escaping through the lifting nozzle at a certain velocity forms a vacuum, or, in other words, sucks the air out of the supply pipe, compelling thereby the water to rise, to fill up the space above its stationary level and to appear at the overflow.

Of course, this cannot be obtained without having the suction pipe and all the connections absolutely air-tight.

As the velocity of steam escaping from an orifice varies with the pressure, the lifting nozzle must be proportioned, so as to be able to lift up the necessary amount of water under the minimum steam pressure. Its lifting capacity depends also on the temperature of the supply water, and the lower the temperature is the better effect it will give.

Below is a table, showing steam pressure, required to lift and deliver water with a No. 6 Sellers *fixed nozzle injector, as obtained from experiments conducted by the

---

*Fixed nozzle injector is one that has nozzles fixed into it, having no motion.

Park Benjamin Scientific Expert Office of New York, during May, 1879.

Height of the lift.		Steam pressure required to lift and deliver water.	Height of the lift.		Steam pressure required to lift and deliver water.
Feet.	Inches.	Lbs. per sq. inch.	Feet.	Inches.	Lbs. per sq. inch.
3	0	25	21	3	52
5	0	30			60
11	6	40	22	10	70
15	0	49			100

From the above it will be seen that no advantage is derived from increasing steam pressure beyond 60 lbs. per sq. inch; while the lift decreases very rapidly when steam pressure is reduced.

In starting a lifting injector, steam is first admitted to the lifting nozzle, the water supply valve having been previously adjusted so as to deliver about the maximum amount of water, corresponding to the steam pressure; and as soon as solid water appears at the overflow, the steam valve of the steam nozzle is opened slightly, until the jet is established, when the full steam pressure is turned on and the steam valve of the lifting nozzle is closed.

The steam valve of the steam nozzle should always be slightly opened before closing the steam valve of the lifting nozzle, in order to prevent a break in the vacuum. Such a break may also occur when the overflow check is closed, breaking off thereby the connection between the stream and the atmosphere, and the water would be forced back through the suction pipe into the tank. This, however, is intentionally done when it is desirable to heat the supply water, and the check valve for this reason is called *heater cock*, which does a good service in the winter time.

NON-LIFTING INJECTOR.

A non-lifting injector is used when there is a head of water or pressure in the hydrant or in the supply reservoir and the water flows into the injector by itself, without being lifted up by the steam jet.

A lifting injector may be converted into a non-lifting by simply closing the steam valve of the lifting nozzle.

THE CONNECTIONS FOR ATTACHING AN INJECTOR.

Like the steam pump, an injector has three connections for attachments and they are respectively known as: *steam, suction* and *delivery* connections, being the only ones, which require attention. They must be made with pipes of the same or greater internal diameter than the openings of the corresponding branches of the injector.

Steam should be taken from the highest part of the boiler, but not on its sides or its ends, in order to avoid the carrying over of water with the steam, as wet steam cuts into and makes grooves in the steam nozzle. In the case of portable or traction engines, it is important to take the steam from the centre of the boiler and at its highest point, as a steam pipe at either end is sure to be flooded with water when ascending or descending a hill. If there is a large pipe for supplying the engine or for any other purpose, the injector's steam pipe is to be placed at a dis-

tance from such pipe, as it will sometimes draw water and
flood the injector's steam pipe, if too close.   It is often
advantageous to provide the boiler with a supplementary
dome, which may simply consist of one foot long piece of
2 inch pipe, and will aid to secure perfectly dry steam.

Suction.—One of the most essential requirements for
the successful working of the injector is a tight suction,
which will not leak air.   This is especially important on a
high lift, and with the smaller sizes of injectors, which in
consequence of their size are perceptibly affected even by
such a small leak, which, perhaps, would not materially
diminish the efficiency of a large injector.   The size of
the suction pipe must be proportional to its length, always
increasing when the lift is high or the trail long, and it
should have as few bends as possible.   There is really no
use for a foot valve, but it is better to place a strainer over
the receiving end of the water supply pipe, in order to
prevent floating particles of wood or any other matter
from being carried up and from clogging the injector.   The
holes in this strainer must not exceed the smallest opening
in the delivery nozzle, and their total area should be
somewhat greater than the area of the water supply
pipe, in order to compensate for some of them becoming
clogged or closed by deposits.   When the supply water
reaches the injector under a head or a pressure, say from
a street main, it is necessary to provide the supply pipe
with a regulating cock or valve, as this pressure may, if
too excessive, disturb the action of the injector.   In such
cases it is always preferable to take the water from a tank
fed by a ball-cock.

Delivery.—The delivery pipe should be as large as called
for by the injector's connection, and a check valve placed
between this connection and boiler, so that the injector
could be disconnected in case of repairs.   The check valve

must be of the same size as the pipe or little larger, as this would not impair the working of the injector.

The *Overflow.*—The overflow must not be piped at all, but a funnel with a drip pipe should be placed under the overflow nozzle so as to carry the waste water into the sewer or collect it into a tank. If it should be found desirable to pipe the overflow, it may be done, but then the overflow pipe must be set as nearly perpendicular as possible, and be larger than the diameter of the overflow. Never allow the outlet of overflow pipe to go below the surface of the water, as this will choke it.

THE BOILER COMPOUND AS A PREVENT-
IVE OF INCRUSTATION AND COR-
ROSION OF INJECTORS.

A great number of Injectors on Locomotive Engines are
supplied with cups for lubricating the interior parts of
Injector to prevent the formation of scale. The cup is
placed at the suction end of the injector as shown on page
42, Fig. 7, and lubricates while the injector is at work.
The quantity of oil is regulated according to the condition
of water.

On railroads, where the water is impure, scale will
appear on the nozzles of an injector, unless precaution is
taken against its formation, so troublesome to the engineer.
Instead of oil it would be much more advantageous to feed
with boiler compound through an injector, as this would
benefit not only the injector alone, but also the boiler.
There is no need of going into details about the danger of
running boilers without proper care, the fact is too well
known to every intelligent engineer, and this alone should
be sufficient for using boiler compounds.

The enormous quantity of this compound consumed an-
nually by all classes of steam boilers shows that so far it is
the only remedy for the prevention of scale in steam
boilers.

Among the many solvents, introduced for the removal
and prevention of scale, the compound manufactured by
Geo. W. Lord, of Philadelphia, Pa., is the only compound
that is not damaging and destructive to boilers, and is the
only chemical preparation that could be used advantage-

ously at the present day. It not only prevents the formation of scale or rot in all kinds of boilers, but also softens
and removes it when it has been already formed without
any injury to the iron, as it neutralizes the action of those
salts, which form the basis of all scale and incrustation.

As the injectors for stationary boilers have no special
arrangements for the introduction of boiler compound, the
same may be added to the feed water, if the latter is obtained from a tank.

SUGGESTIONS TO ENGINEERS.

Engineers are sometimes experiencing considerable difficulties in trying to find out the cause that their injector fails to work and attempt to interfere with the interior of the injector.

In many cases the trouble lies in the connections and therefore it is advisable to examine them, before disconnecting the injector.

In making pipe connections, it is necessary to blow them out clean, before connecting the injector, in order to wash out all red lead, scale or other solids, that may be in the pipes and which would otherwise fill the nozzles of the injector and impair its action. After the connections have been examined and found in good order, the injector is disconnected and the cap or plug removed for cleaning the nozzles.

1. WHEN THE INJECTOR FAILS TO LIFT the water well the difficulty is with the suction, which must be absolutely airtight.

2. The cause may also be with the overflow. When the latter is choked or piped, and is not wide open, the steam and air do not have a free vent, and would not let the water rise.

3. When the supply pipe is very hot, it should be cooled off with cold water or by letting the steam on and off suddenly at the starting valve, until the hot water is all disposed of.

4. When the lift is out of proportion to the steam pressure, and the steam pressure is either too low or too high.

5. Absence of water at the supply source.

6. The strainer may be clogged up.

WHEN AN INJECTOR LIFTS THE WATER BUT DOES NOT FORCE IT TO THE BOILER.

1. In many cases this trouble is caused by starving the injector, *i. e.*, by not giving it enough water.

2. Through a defective check valve in the delivery pipe, which may be stuck down, or is not set properly and does not rise sufficiently.

3. By a leak in the supply pipe, admitting air to the injector along with the supply water.

4. By the delivery nozzle having become dirty, and it must be cleaned in the manner prescribed in the description of each kind of injector.

IF THE INJECTOR STARTS BUT "BREAKS."

1. The supply water is not properly regulated.

2. A leak in the supply pipe admits air into the injector.

3. The disc of the steam valve may be loose.

4. Connecting steam pipe to a pipe used for other purposes.

DIRECTIONS FOR DETERMINING THE PROPER SIZE OF INJECTORS.

Knowing the number of cubic feet of water evaporated per hour by a boiler, the proper size of injector to supply it may be determined from the table of capacities furnished by manufacturers of injectors.

Given the indicated horse power, the quantity of water required may be approximately obtained, assuming that each horse power requires one cubic foot of water per hour, which is equivalent to 7½ gallons, and by multiplying the number of horse power of boiler by the number of gallons. The product will be the amount of water required for the boiler per hour, and the table of capacities will give the size of the injector. In no case, should the injector selected be larger than will give at maximum pressure the number of cubic feet of water, corresponding to the number of horse power; for, if too large, the minimum may exceed the wants of the boiler, necessitating frequent stoppages in order to prevent flooding, which, aside from the trouble it occasions, is not so economical as a constant and regular feed, exactly compensating the drain on the boiler.

USEFUL INFORMATION.

A cubic foot of water contains 7½ gallons U. S. Standard and weighs 62½ pounds.

The U. S. Standard gallon measures 231 cubic inches and contains 8½ lbs. of distilled water.

To evaporate one cubic foot of water requires the consumption of 7½ lbs. of coal; or about 1 lb. of coal to one gallon of water.

The average consumption of coal for steam boilers is 12 lbs. per hour for each square foot of grate.

U. S. Gallons multiplied by 231 will express the volume in cubic inches.

A cubic inch of water evaporated under ordinary atmospheric pressure is converted into one cubic foot of steam.

Steam at atmospheric pressure flows into a vacuum at the rate of about 1550 feet per second, and into the atmosphere at the rate of 650 feet per second.

The specific gravity of steam (at atmospheric pressure) is .411 of that of air at 34° Fah., and .0006 of that of water at same temperature.

27,222 cubic feet of steam weigh 1 pound.

11,188 cubic feet of air weigh one pound.

Locomotives average a consumption of 3000 gallons of water per one hundred miles.

To remove lime, when the nozzles of an injector become coated with it, let them stand over night in a solution of one part of Muriatic acid to 10 parts water; or boil the nozzles in vinegar and salt, using two table-spoonfuls of salt to one quart of vinegar.

TABLE OF FLOW OF STEAM THROUGH PIPES.

Initial pressure by Gauge lbs. per sq. in	Diameter of Pipe in Inches.								Length of each = 240 diameters.					
	¾	1	1½	2	2½	3	4	5	6	8	10	12	15	18
	Weight of Steam per minute in pounds, with 1 pound loss of pressure.													
1	1.16	2.07	5.7	10.27	15.45	25.38	46.85	77.3	115.9	211.4	341.1	502.4	804	1177
10	1.44	2.57	7.1	12.72	19.15	31.45	58.05	95.8	143.6	262.0	422.7	622.5	996	1458
20	1.70	3.02	8.3	14.94	22.49	36.94	68.20	112.6	168.7	307.8	496.5	731.3	1170	1713
30	1.91	3.40	9.4	16.84	25.35	41.63	76.84	126.9	190.1	346.8	559.5	824.1	1318	1930
40	2.10	3.74	10.3	18.51	27.87	45.77	84.49	139.5	209.0	381.3	615.3	906.0	1450	2122
50	2.27	4.04	11.2	20.01	30.13	49.48	91.34	150.8	226.0	412.2	665.0	979.5	1567	2294
60	2.43	4.32	11.9	21.38	32.19	52.87	97.60	161.1	241.5	440.5	710.6	1046.7	1675	2451
70	2.57	4.58	12.6	22.65	34.10	56.00	103.37	170.7	255.8	466.5	752.7	1108.5	1774	2596
80	2.71	4.82	13.3	23.82	35.87	58.91	108.74	179.5	269.0	490.7	791.7	1166.1	1866	2731
90	2.83	5.04	13.9	24.92	37.52	61.62	113.74	187.8	281.4	513.3	828.1	1219.8	1951	2856
100	2.95	5.25	14.5	25.96	39.07	64.18	118.47	195.6	293.1	534.6	862.6	1270.1	2032	2975
120	3.16	5.63	15.5	27.85	41.93	68.87	127.12	209.9	314.5	573.7	925.6	1363.3	2181	3193
150	3.45	6.14	17.0	30.37	45.72	75.09	138.61	228.8	343.0	625.5	1009.2	1486.5	2378	3481

For horse-power, multiply the figures in the table by 2. For any other loss of pressure, multiply by the square root of the given loss.

A horse-power in a steam-engine or other prime mover, is 550 lbs. raised 1 foot per second, or 33,000 lbs. 1 foot per minute.

INJECTORS

ADAPTED FOR

LOCOMOTIVE BOILER SERVICE

·

EXPLANATION OF DETAILS.

DIRECTIONS FOR OPERATION.

SELLERS' SELF-ACTING LIFTING INJECTOR OF 1887.

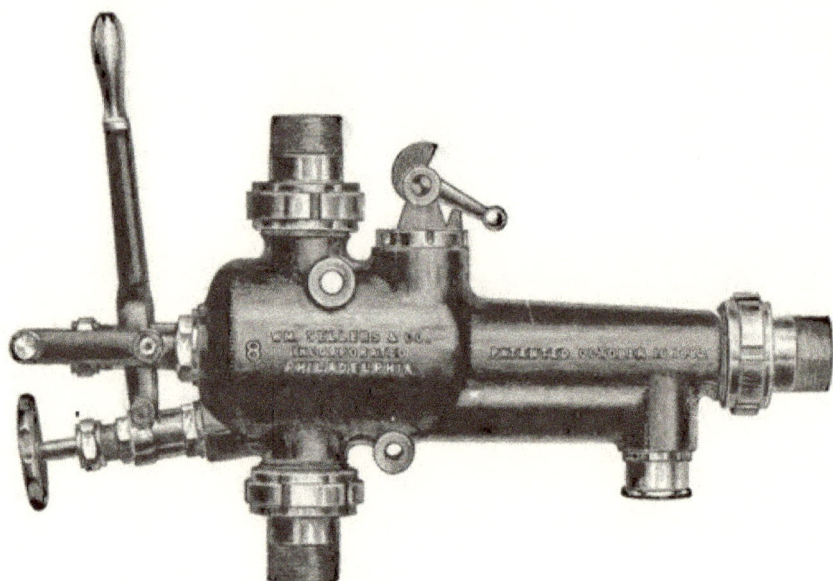

Fig. 1.

The accompanying engravings represent an elevation and sectional view of Sellers' self-acting injector of 1887. Referring to Fig. 2, the sectional view of the injector, it will be seen it consists of case A provided with a steam inlet B, a water inlet C, an outlet D through which the water is conveyed to the boiler, an overflow opening E, a lever F by which to admit steam, start and stop its working, a hand wheel G to regulate the supply of water, and an eccentric lever H to close the waste valve when it is desired to make a heater of the injector.

The operation of the injector is as follows: The water inlet C being in communication with the water supply, the valve *a* is opened to allow the water to enter the chamber I. Steam is admitted to the chamber B and the lever F is drawn out to lift the valve *b* from its seat and permit the steam to enter the annular lifting steam nozzle *c* through the holes *d d*. The issuing steam from this nozzle passes through the annular combining tube *e* and escapes from the instrument partly through the overflow opening *f* and

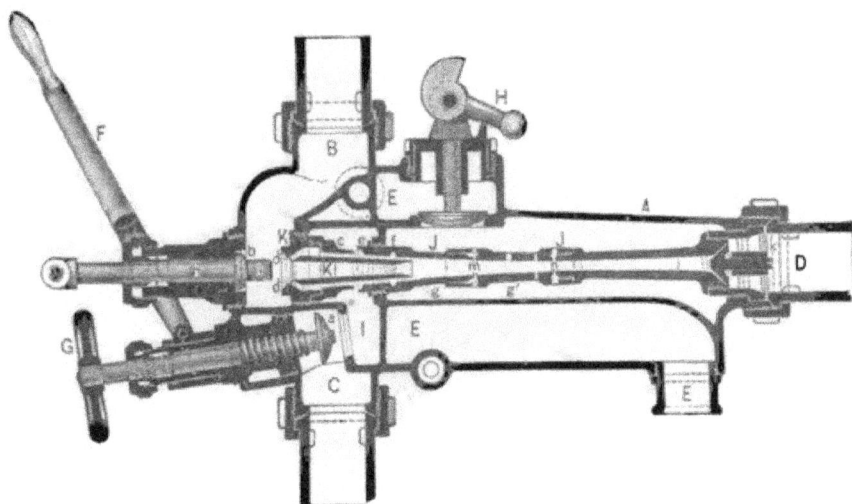

Fig. 2.

partly through the overflow openings provided in the combining tube *g g*, through the overflow chamber J and passage E E, and produces a strong vacuum in the water chamber I, which lifts the water from the source of supply, and the united jet of steam and water is by reason of its velocity, discharged into the rear of receiving end of the combining tube *g*. The further movement of the lever F withdraws the spindle *h* until the steam plug *i* is out of the steam nozzle K, allowing the steam to pass through the steam nozzle K and come in contact with the annular jet of water which is flowing into the combining nozzle around the nozzle K. This jet of water has already considerable velocity, and the forcing steam jet imparts to it the necessary increment of velocity to enable it to enter the boiler through the delivery nozzle J and check *k*.

THE SELLERS' NON-LIFTING INJECTOR.

The non-lifting injector, which is shown in the figs. 3 and 4, is more simple in construction and in operation than the one just described. It is generally placed below the level of the water in the tender.

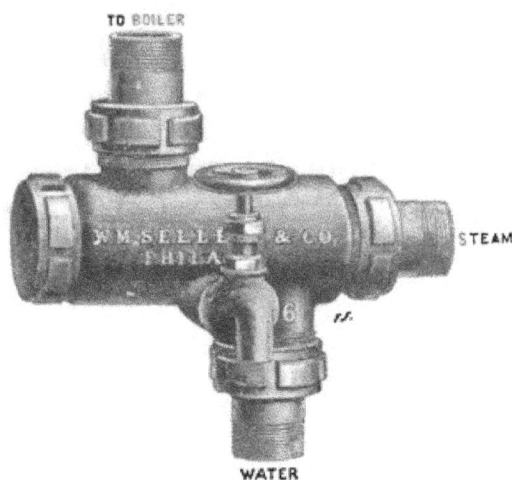

Fig. 3.

To start the injector it is necessary to open the water supply valve sufficiently to deliver about the maximum amount of water that the injector can take at the given pressure, and, the overflow valve being open, as soon as the water escapes freely through the overflow, to open the steam valve slightly, until the jet is established, and then to open the steam valve wide by a quick motion. The quantity of water is regulated by a special water valve.

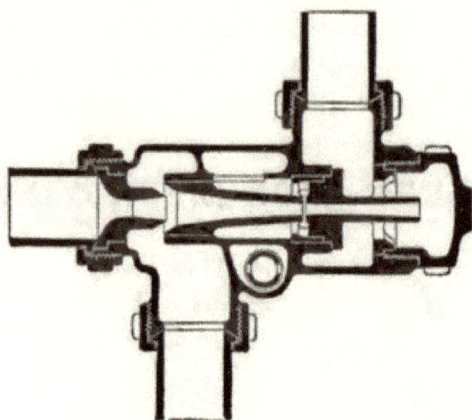

Fig. 4.

The nozzles of the lifting injector as well as of the non-lifting, are fixed in a straight line, so that a wire can readily be passed through them to dislodge an obstruction if necessary, by simply disconnecting the pipe union in the delivery end of the former or the cap of the latter.

FRIEDMANN'S PATENT LIFTING INJECTOR.
THE MONITOR OF 1888.

Figs. 5 and 6 represent an elevation and sectional view of the injector, the construction and operation of which may be described as follows:

Referring to Fig. 6, it will be seen that the injector consists of a case, provided with a steam outlet, water inlet and an outlet, through which the water is forced into the boiler, an overflow opening, a lever by which to admit steam, start and stop its working, a hand wheel to regulate the supply of water, and a T handle to close the waste valve, when it is desired to make a heater of the injector.

A hollow spindle (called the lifting nozzle), passing through the steam nozzle into the combining nozzle, is secured to a rod and valve. A second valve is secured to the same rod in such a manner that it can be opened (thus admitting steam to the centre of the spindle,) without raising the former valve (of the steam nozzle) from its seat, if the rod is not drawn out any farther, after the stop on the hollow spindle comes in contact with the valve. The rod is connected to a cross-head, which is lifted over the guide rod, and a lever is secured to the cross-head.

The manipulation required to start the injector is as follows: Move lever until contact takes place between the valve and the stop on hollow spindle, which can be felt by the hand upon the lever, steam is admitted to the centre of the spindle, and expanding as it passes into the condensing and overflow nozzles lifts the water through the supply pipe into the combining nozzle. As soon as solid

water appears at the overflow the lever may be drawn out
to its full extent, opening the steam valve of the steam

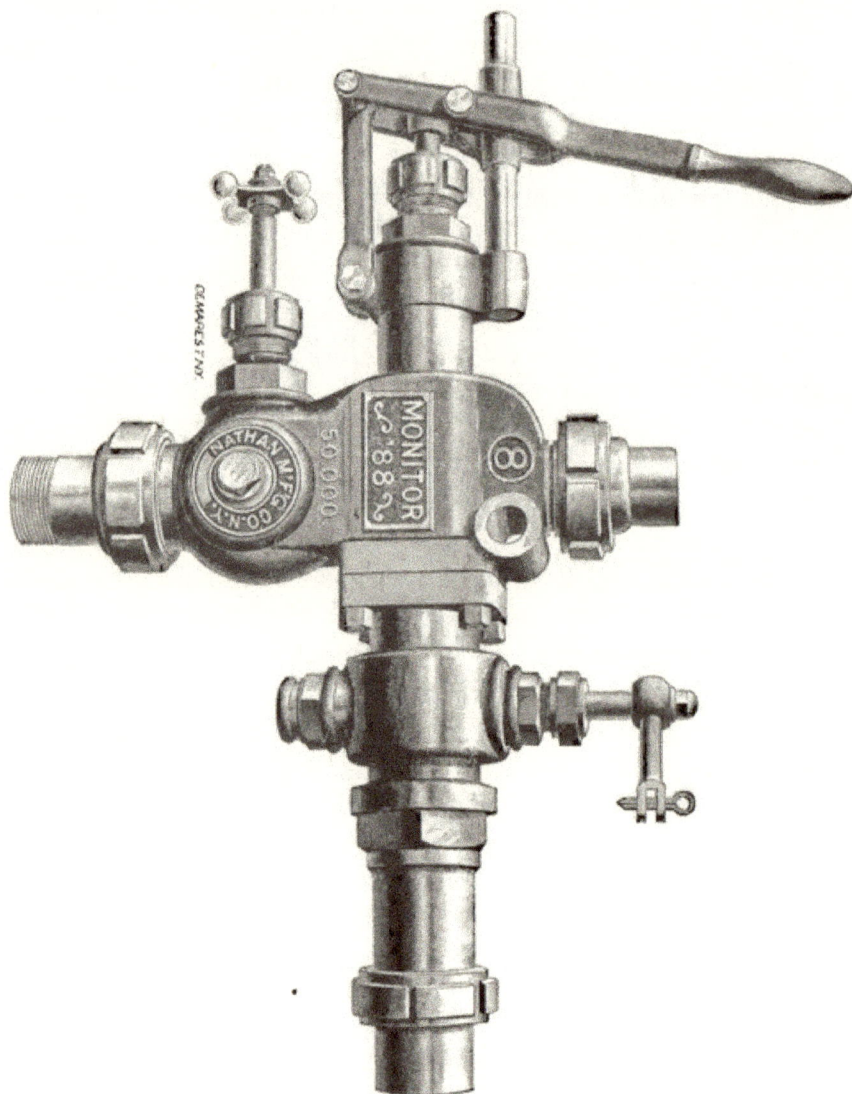

nozzle when the action of the injector will be continuous
as long as steam and water are supplied to it.   To regu-

late the amount of water delivered at different pressures of steam turn the hand wheel to right or left, thus closing or opening the water valve.

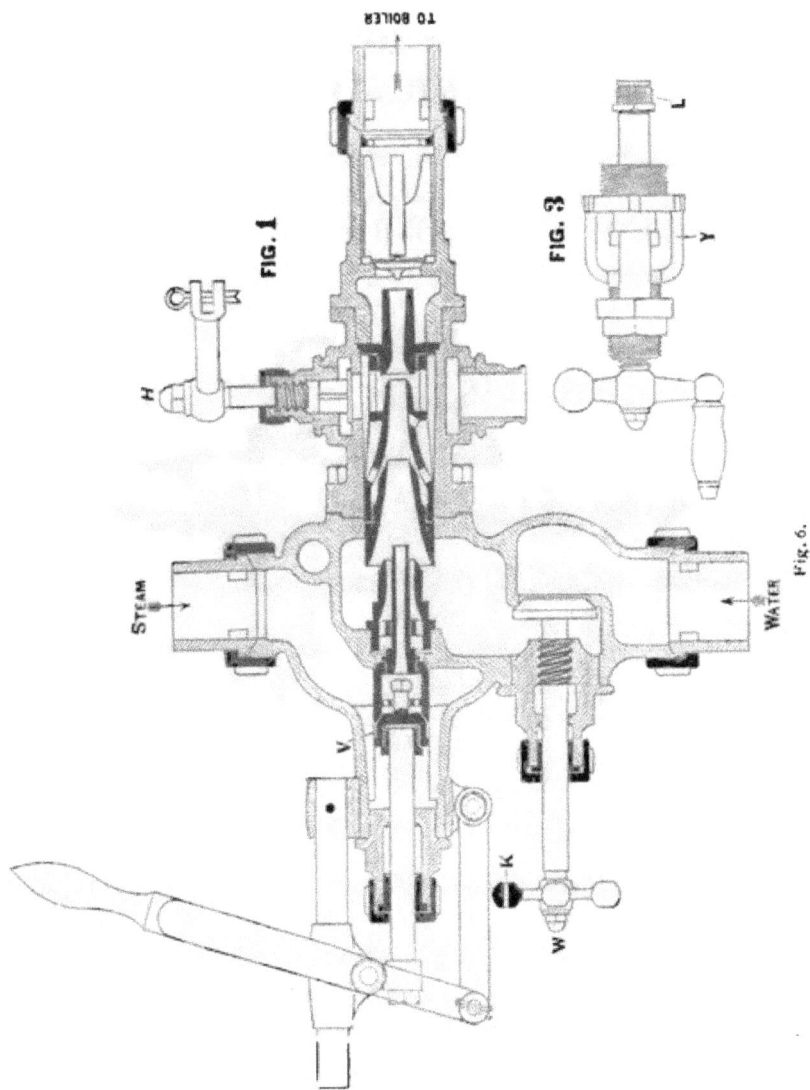

THE REGULAR MONITOR LIFTING INJECTOR.

The accompanying engravings represent the same Monitor injector as already described on the preceding page, with that difference that the regular Monitor injector has an independent lifting jet.

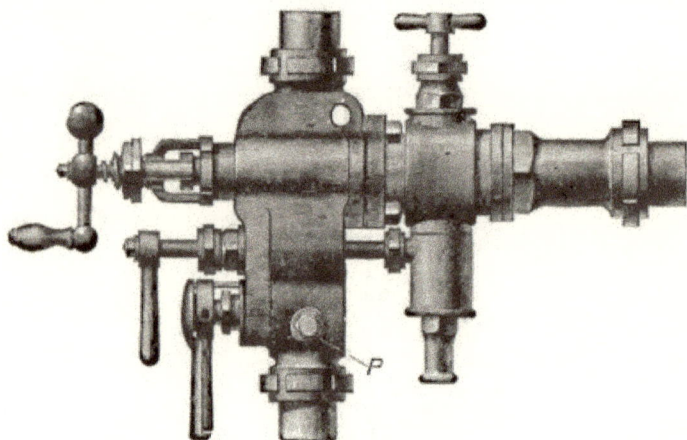

Fig. 7.

To start this injector open jet valve J first when water appears at overflow, open steam valve which is situated above the jet and close jet valve.

The steam valve should always be slightly opened before closing the jet valve, so as to prevent a break in the vacuum.

The nozzles are easily reached by unscrewing the line check L as shown on Fig. 8.

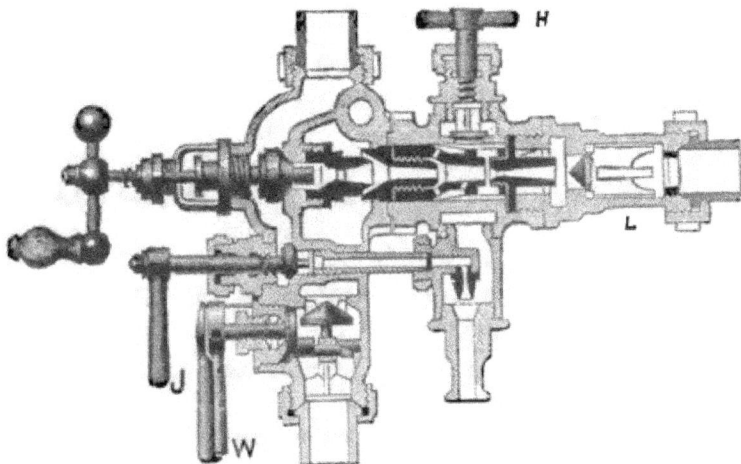

Fig. 8.

The position of the Monitor injector on a locomotive engine is shown on the following Fig. 9.

Fig. 9.

THE W. F. NON-LIFTING INJECTOR.

The class W. F. non-lifting injector, represented in Figs. 10 and 11, is a modification of the original Friedmann injector of Vienna. It is capable of regulating the water supply to meet the demands of the engine under different pressures and rates of speed.

It is operated by simply opening and closing the steam valve in starting and stopping. The feed water may be reduced to more than half the capacity of the injector by

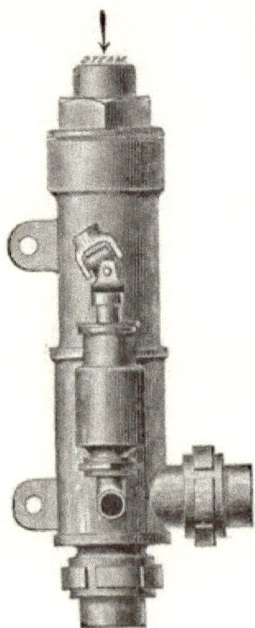

Fig. 10.

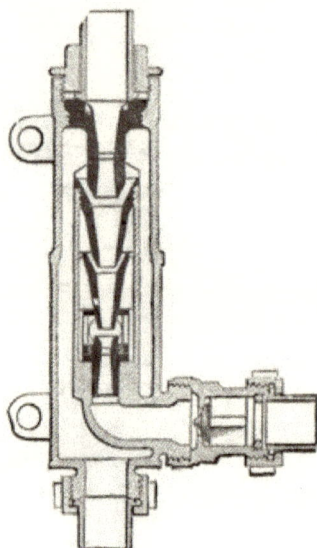

Fig. 11.

44

partially closing the lazy-cock placed in the supply pipe
between the injector and tender of engine.

The position of this injector on a locomotive is shown
in Fig. 12.

Fig. 12.

GARFIELD'S AUTOMATIC LIFTING INJECTOR.

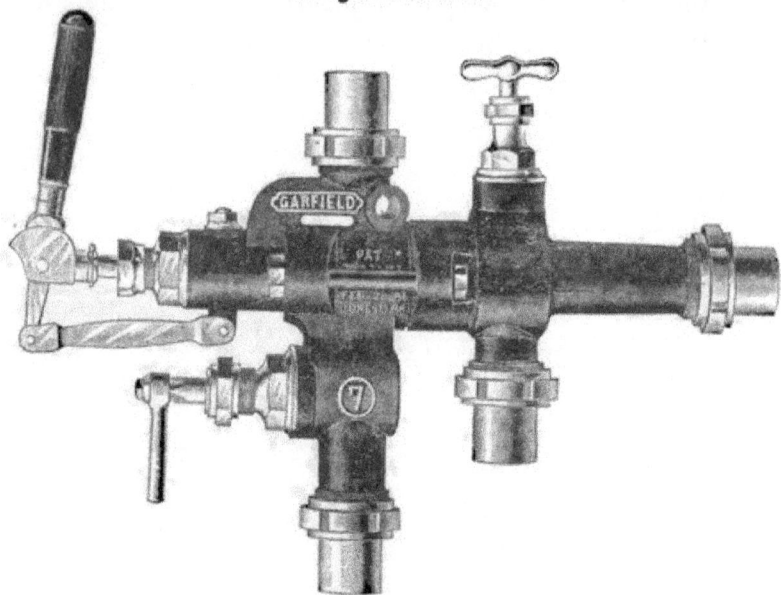

Fig. 13.

The above engraving represents the Garfield injector recently patented and introduced. The construction and position of the nozzles is shown in the Figure 14 below. The action of the steam and water in the combined nozzle where they come together at 2 and 3 is to form a vacuum

Fig. 14.

or to expel all the air from the chambers designated.
When this vacuum forms, the ring 5 adheres closely to the
condensing chamber. Whenever this vacuum is broken,
the stream of water forced into the boiler is also broken,
and should the stream from any cause be broken by being
graded **very low, or** from any motion of **the engine** in passing over a rough track, **it is** easily restarted.

The manipulation required to start the injector is as follows: Open steam valve by moving the lever out forward,
then regulate the water valve by the **handle** underneath
the lever.

The nozzles are easily reached by unscrewing the bolts,
and when the injector is put together, care should be taken
to have the nozzles put in as they are shown in the cut
above, and that the bolts are tightened evenly **so as** to
properly seat the nozzles.

KORTING UNIVERSAL LIFTING INJECTOR
OF 1889.

The accompanying engravings represent the external and internal views of the Korting injector, used for either locomotive or stationary boilers. The instrument is a combination of two steam jet apparatuses, the first one proportioned for lifting and delivering the water, under some pressure into the second one, where its velocity is sufficiently augmented to overcome the counter pressure

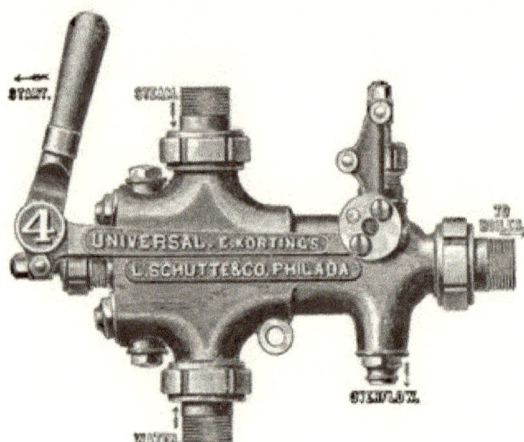

Fig. 15.

in the boiler. The first apparatus has a proportionately small steam nozzle, to insure high suction. The nozzles are easily removed for cleaning or repairing by unscrewing the caps K K K K, and when putting them in, attention must be paid to have them placed into the same position,

48

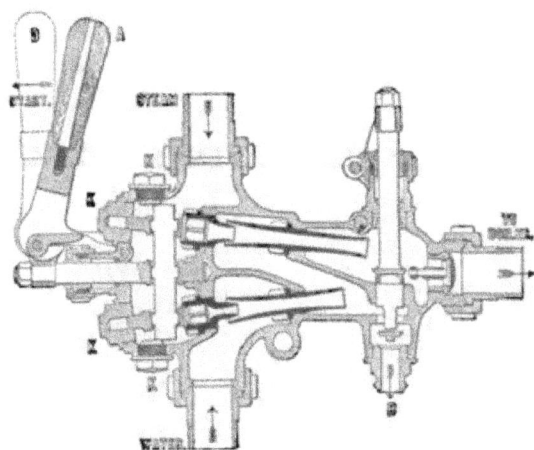

Fig. 16.

and for that purpose the lower nozzles are marked L, and the upper ones U (stamped on casting).

To start the injector open steam valves by moving the lever A Fig. 16 to the direction of the arrow as shown by the dotted lines.

Fig. 17.

In Fig. 17 is shown the position of the injector on locomotive engine.

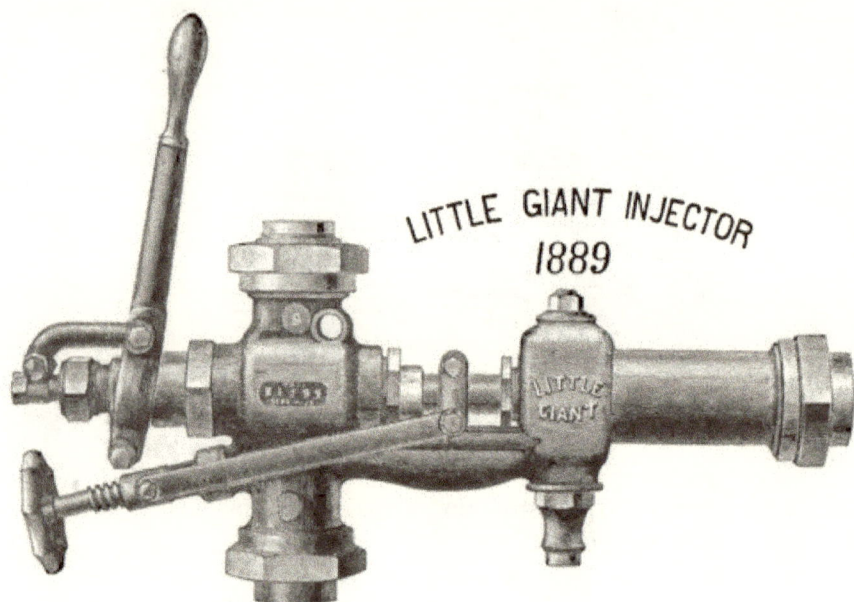

Fig. 18.

The above engraving represents an improvement of the Little Giant lifting injector, shown in Fig. 19. The regulation of the quantity of water supplied to the injector is performed by the hand wheel, Fig. 18, which being secured to the combining nozzle, moves the latter towards A and B, fig. 19, thus reducing or enlarging the space between the steam nozzle and the combining nozzle, allowing a large quantity of water to enter when moved towards B, and a smaller quantity towards A.

This arrangement can be seen from the sectional view of a stationary injector, represented in Fig. 41, page 69.

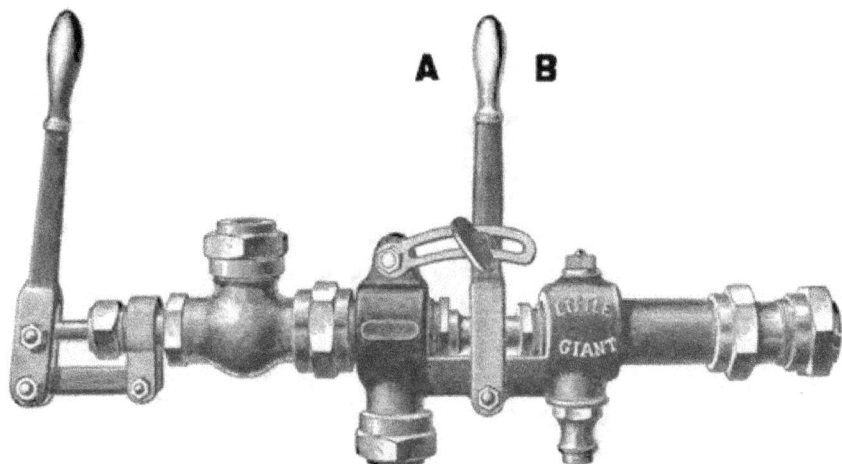

A   B

Fig. 19.

To start injector, have the combining tube or nozzle in position to allow sufficient water to condense the steam when starting valve is wide open.   Then open the starting valve slightly; when water shows at overflow open starting valve wide, where it should remain while injector is at work. The quantity of water is graduated by moving the combining nozzle.

To stop injector, close starting valve.

When the injector is to be used as a Heater, to heat the water in the tender, close overflow by moving combining nozzle towards the discharge, and open the steam valve to admit steam.

The nozzles are easily reached for cleaning by removing the delivery end coupling and the front steam valve.

NON-LIFTING LITTLE GIANT.

The non-lifting injector represented in Fig. 20 and 21 elevation and sectional views is generally placed below the level of the water in tender.   As seen from the cuts it is a

Fig. 20.

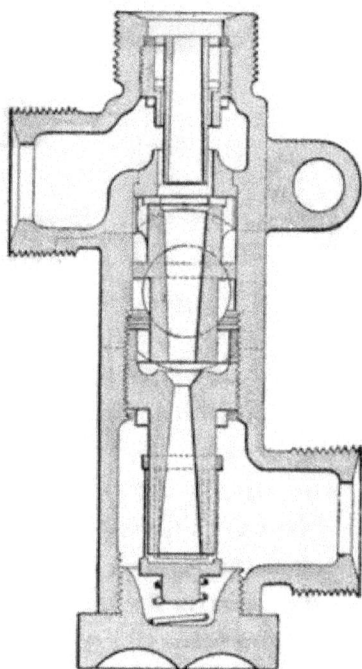

Fig. 21.

very simple instrument and its parts easily to be removed for repair, by simply unscrewing the cap at the bottom of the machine.

THE HANCOCK INSPIRATOR.

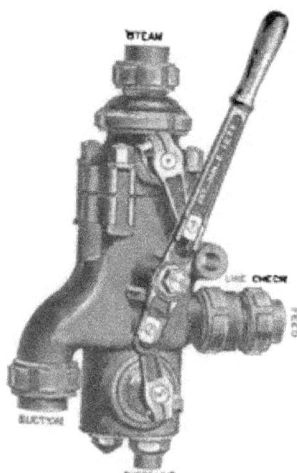

Fig. 22.

The word Inspirator has been applied to the machine by its inventor, Mr. John T. Hancock, M. E., who has been dead some years.

The inspirator is a similar instrument to an injector and differs only in its construction. The inspirator shown in the above cut is similar to the one already described on page 48. It consists of a double apparatus, one-half of which is a lifter, and the other half a forcer, the lifter drawing the water and delivering it to the forcer, which delivers it to the boiler, at any steam pressure, without adjustment. A sectional cut of this injector applied to stationary boilers is shown in Fig. 37, page 67.

To start the inspirator, draw the lever back sufficiently to bring the water, then draw it back to the stop.

INJECTORS

ADAPTED FOR

Stationary Boiler Service.

EXPLANATION OF DETAILS.

DIRECTION FOR OPERATION.

N. B.—Injectors for Stationary Boilers differ from the ones adapted for Locomotive Boiler service only in the dimension of their respective internal parts ;
the former being constructed to perform the duty under a considerably lower
steam pressure than the latter.

FRIEDMANN'S PATENT INJECTORS.

THE MONITOR LIFTING INJECTOR.

Figures 23 and 24 represent an elevation and sectional view of the Monitor lifting injector, which is an adaptation of the well known locomotive injector of that name to stationary boilers, and possesses all the characteristics of that splendid instrument, a description of which has already

Fig. 23.

been given on page 42. These injectors are also capable of being worked down to half their capacity by regulating with water valve only. This injector may also be used as a non-lifting where a head of water is available.

To start the injector: Open jet valve J until the water

flows out of the overflow O, as soon as the water appears at the overflow, open the main steam valve, and close the jet valve J.

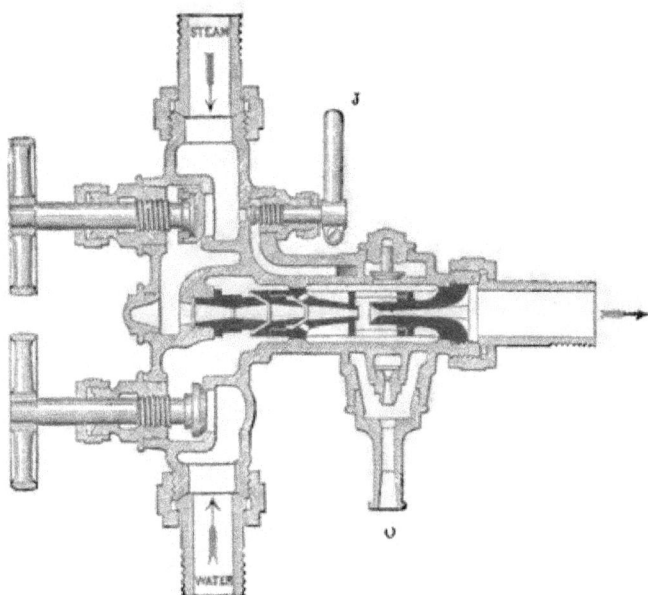

Fig. 24.

Should water still be discharged from the overflow, reduce gradually the water supply by water valve until the discharge ceases.

THE MONITOR NON-LIFTING INJECTOR.

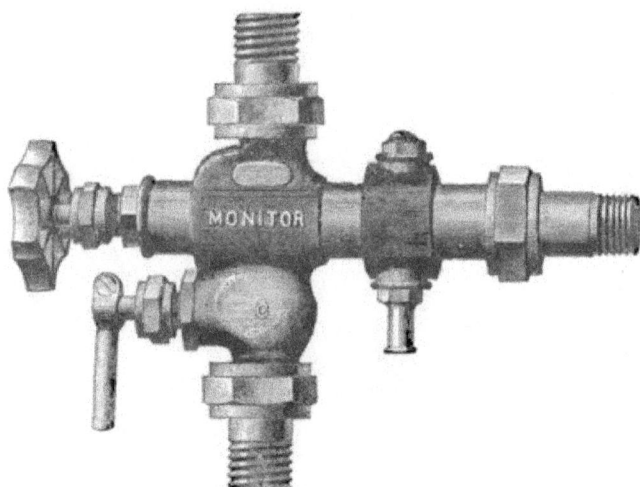

Fig. 25.

The injector represented in the above cut is the same as the Monitor lifting injector, with the exception of the lifting jet, which, in this injector, is dispensed with, and consequently the manipulation required to start the non-lifting injector is the same as the one for the lifting injector, the lifting jet valve not being considered.

THE PENBERTHY AUTOMATIC LIFTING INJECTOR.

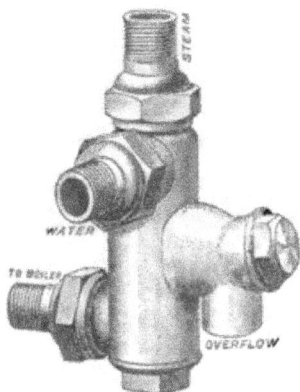

Fig. 26.

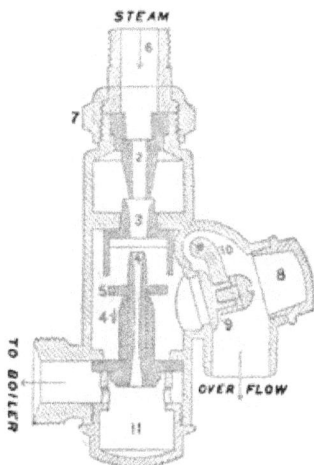

Fig. 27.

The above figures represent an elevation and sectional view of the improved Penberthy Automatic Injector. Refering to Fig. 27 it will be seen that the action of the steam and water, when they meet at 2 and 3, is the same as in the injector described on pages 46 and 60, viz: the ring 5 adheres closely to 3 as soon as the vacuum is formed by the action of the steam and water at 2 and 3, expelling the air out of those chambers.

To start the injector: Open the globe valve on steam end and then globe valve in water supply pipe. If water continues to issue from overflow after injector has started, throttle the water valve until the discharge ceases.

To stop: Close the steam valve. The water valve need not be closed unless the injector is used as a non-lifter.

GRESHAM'S AUTOMATIC INJECTOR.

The following cuts, Figs. 28 and 29, represent the Gresham's new patent automatic re-starting injector. This injector has taken the first prize in the Inventors' Exhibition in London, and was the most interesting feature of the machinery department of that exhibition, and was selected by the managers to supply the boilers which furnished the steam for the motive power used in the exhibition. Among its most valuable points were its instantaneous and per-

Fig. 28.

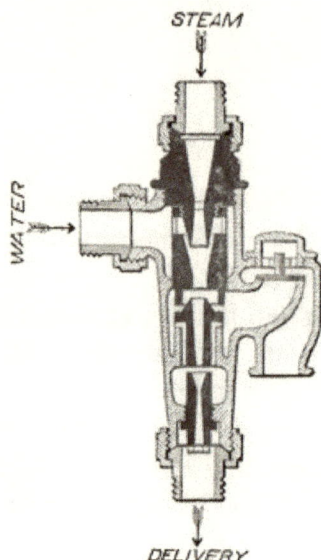

Fig. 29.

fectly automatic performance as soon as steam and water were turned on, and its restarting quality, which enabled it to take up the feed water at once and without any handling

of valves, after the supply had been withdrawn or inter-
rupted from any cause whatsoever. The last feature seems
to make the Gresham injector peculiarly adapted for the
feed of boilers of traction engines and tug boats, and
steam craft generally, where the supply of feed water is so
liable to interruption from traveling over rough surfaces
on the one hand, and from the motion of the waves on the
other.

To start injector, open steam valve first and then the
water valve in the supply pipe. If water continues to issue
from overflow after the injector had started, turn back the
water valve until the discharge ceases.

To stop, close steam valve. The water need not be
closed unless the injector is used as a non-lifter.

SELLERS' FIXED NOZZLE AUTOMATIC LIFTING INJECTOR OF 1885.

Fig. 30.

The above illustration represent the Sellers Fixed Nozzle Automatic Injector for feeding stationary boilers. It can be used either to receive the water supply under a head, or raise it a considerable height before delivering it into the boiler. By reference to the sectional view Fig. 31, A is the body; B, steam connection; C, water supply connection, in which is situated the water regulating valve R; D is the water delivery connection containing a check-valve, and leading to the boiler. The overflow valve N may be shifted to either side of the injector's body, and turned radially, so that the injector may be placed in any position that will permit to discharge the overflow vertically downward.

By removing the end caps all of the nozzles can be removed for examination or for cleaning without disturbing the pipe connections.

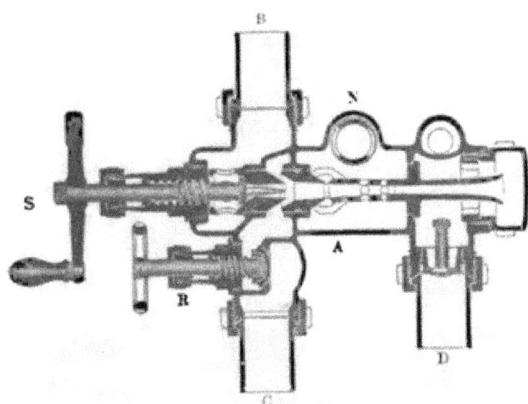

Fig. 31.

The manipulation required to start, when feed water is to be raised: Open steam valve S one-half turn, and when water appears at the overflow open steam valve until overflow ceases.

When feed water is under pressure: Open 1st water regulating valve R; 2d, open steam valve S all the way. Regulate the supply by the water valve R.

KORTING UNIVERSAL INJECTOR OF 1886.

SIDE LEVER STYLE.

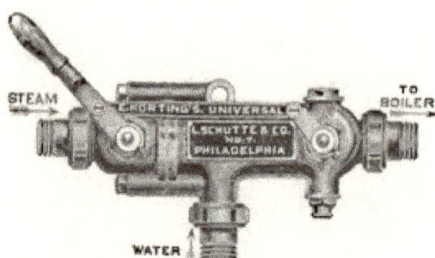

Fig. 32.

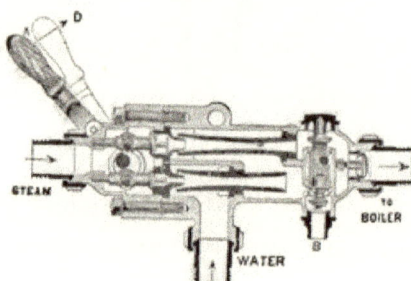

Fig. 33.

A similar injector with an improved front lever has been described on page 48. The object of the above illustrations is to show the construction of this class of injector, a great number of which are in use at present.

The position of the injector attached to a stationary boiler is represented on the figure below, and shows the manner in which the lifting and non-lifting injectors are connected to a steam boiler.

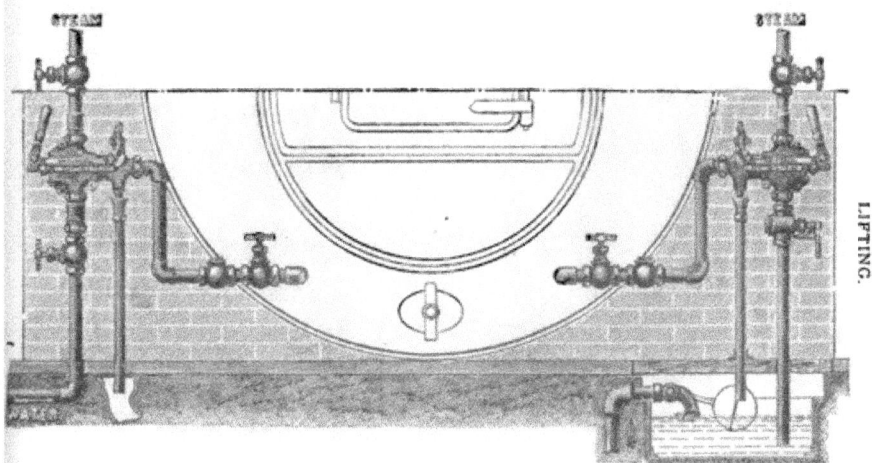

THE AMERICAN AUTOMATIC INJECTOR.

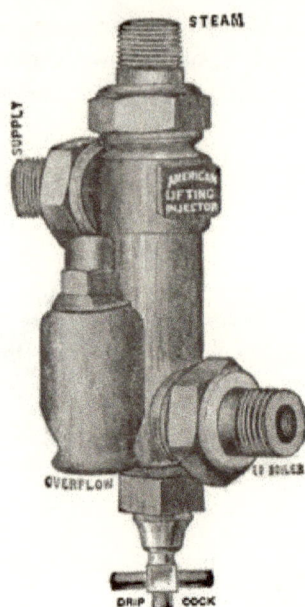

Fig. 34.

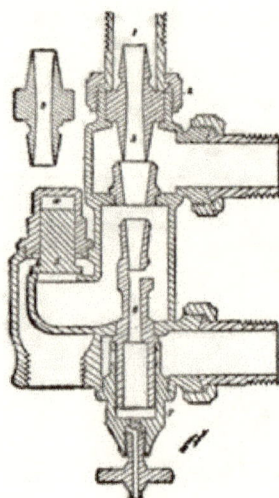

Fig. 35.

The inventor of the above injector, Mr. H. Murdock, has invented the first automatic live steam injector made in this country. The injector, however, was not exactly similar to the machine shown in the Figs. 34 and 35, which was patented in Jan. 12, 1886.

The injector is operated by opening the steam valve first and then the valve in the supply (or suction pipe). The injector is controlled entirely by the valve in supply pipe, after steam is turned on. By means of this valve the injector is made to throw its maximum and minimum of water, and may also be given too much as well as too little water.

THE HANCOCK INSPIRATOR.

Fig. 36.

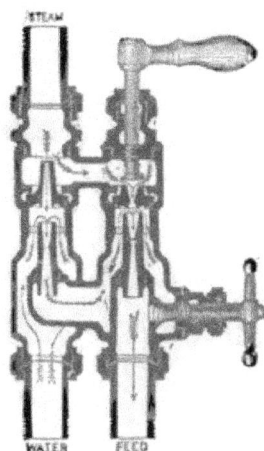

Fig. 37.

The action of this inspirator can easily be understood by following the direction of the arrows, as shown in the sectional cut, Fig. 37.

This class of inspirator is employed for feeding stationary boilers. Its construction and action has been already given on page 53.

THE EBERMAN LIFTING INJECTOR.

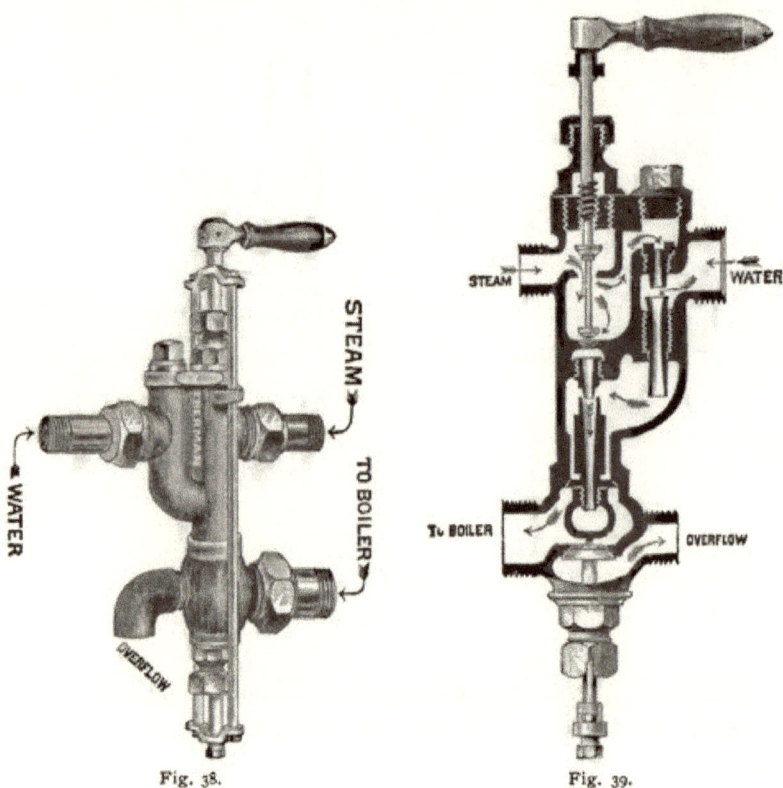

Fig. 38.

Fig. 39.

The above engravings show the elevation and sectional view of a boiler feeder invented by Mr. Albert Eberman. Looking at the sectional view, Fig. 39, it will be seen that the action of this injector is very similar to the one described on page 64. To start the injector turn the handle one-quarter, or less, to lift, waiting until water comes at overflow and gets cool, then pass the handle on around until the overflow is closed; then the feeder is at work.

THE LITTLE GIANT NON-LIFTING INJECTOR.

Fig. 40.

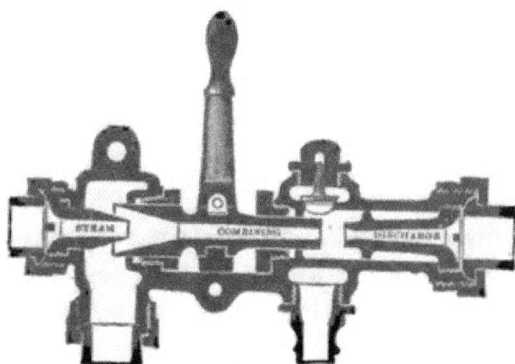

Fig. 41.

These injectors are similar to the Locomotive Little Giant, only they have no lever starting valve, and when the water is to be raised a lifter is placed in the water pipe, with an independent jet, which permits the use of ordinary valves in place of special ones. The manipulation required to operate these injectors is the same as for the locomotive injector described on page 50.

INJECTOR AS A FIRE EXTINGUISHER.

We have already mentioned, at the beginning of this work, that the principle of injectors has numerous other applications and that all its other uses, except as a boiler feeder, were foreign to our programme. However, we find it desirable to make a short deviation, having taken in consideration, that it is almost within the personal experience and observation of every steam engineer, that in cases of a big conflagration the resources of the fire department, turns to be insufficient and that in such localities where fire apparatuses do not exist at all; the relief is sought from those, who are in charge of steam boilers and are near enough to be able to render an efficient service.

Moreover, it would not be unreasonable to expect, that the safety of the establishment, where the engineer operates, is of the greatest personal interest to him, and that he must be the first and the most competent person to give an immediate relief, as far as the means at his hands afford, in case of fire. In fact, it must be his sacred duty to be always prepared for such an emergency, and not to wait for the arrival of the outside help, but be ready to do his best at a moments notice. These considerations, namely, make us believe, that a few words about injectors use for fire extinguishing purposes would not be out of place here.

Fire engineers were always anxiously looking for some means or methods of increasing the efficiency of their apparatuses, especially in those cases where the head on the hydrant was not great and the engine could not force water to the desired height. The principle of injector has not escaped their attention, and they readily understood, as Mr. Froude observes, "that any surface which in passing through a fluid experience resistance, must in doing so impress on the particles, which resist it, a force in the line of motion, equal to the resistance. This, of course, applies as much to a stream of water, as to a solid surface, and in that case as much force is communicated to the slow moving fluid, as is taken out of the rapid stream, although, some of the effects must necessarily be lost in eddies and whirls." It was soon found out, however, that this loss was insignificant, when compared to the many advantages which the utilization of this principle would necessarily possess, and how it could considerably increase the height of the stream thrown out of the fire engines.

These considerations have induced Messrs. Martindale and Greathead to design their hydrant injectors, which are arranged differently in order to make them best suited for the work under varying conditions.

In the opinion of the chiefs of fire department, the maximum quantity of water required for extinguishing fires would be 2000 gallons per one minute, divided between fourteen jets, passing through an aggregate of half of a mile of hose, or of two hundred feet of its length for each jet. If the hose is about 2½ inches in diameter, it requires 3 inches of head for every running foot, so that 50 feet of head will be absorbed by the jet, and if the pressure in the hydrant is 32 lbs. per square inch, the same is equivalent to 74 feet head of water.

It is easy to understand, how injector can be utilized for the purposes of extinguishing. The principle remaining the same, its application to the fire apparatuses differs from its use for feeding steam boilers in this, that while in the latter case the liquified jet of steam issuing from the delivery nozzle, was calculated so as to be strong enough to force its way into the boiler, after having lifted the check valve, and to lose all its momentum as soon as it had spread out and mingled itself with the hot water inside of the boiler, in the case of extinguishing fire this jet issuing from the delivery nozzle must possess a velocity in the same direction, in which the water, it impinges upon, flows and be greater than that of the latter, in order to be able to carry it along and to a greater height, than it could rise itself without this assistance.

The velocity, of course, depends upon the pressure of the steam in the boiler, and consequently can be easily obtained by attending to the firing of the boiler and by consulting the steam gauge. As to the direction, it must be regulated by making the geometrical axis of the delivery nozzle fall with the line of motion of the extinguishing jet, or what amounts to the same, with the direction of the hose.

This condition can be easily satisfied by making a suitable connection of the hydrant with the hose by means of a double bend and by coupling the injector right opposite to the hose. As a matter of course, the double bend must have besides the two end openings, (one for the hydrant, and one for the hose) a third one for the injector connection. From this it is easy to see, that the utilization of injector for fire extinguishing purposes does not present any difficulty, and an intelligent engineer can always provide himself with whatever is necessary beforehand, so that, if he has a spare injector of a large size, he would be able to use it for that end without a moments delay.

The arrangement as regards the details must be left to his own judgment, as it will vary according to circumstances, and will principally depend upon the **source of** water supply, **i. e.,** wether the same is obtained from the street main, from a cistern, from a well or from **a river, etc.** When a boiler is supplied with two injectors or when there is a reserve steam boiler with a separate injector, attached to it, the engineer **can** always **have those injectors in** readiness for immediate use in **case of** fire. However, **it would be much more convenient to be provided with an extra injector for** that purpose **and all necessary connections.**

Concerning the efficiency of injector **as a fire extinguishing** appliance, **we can** affirm without **hesitation, on the strength of numerous reports of experts, that the same turns to be very satisfactory.** The liquified jet is capable of carrying along with it double **of its own volume of** water with a comparatively speaking small loss **of its own** velocity. The **fact that the most of the locomotive engines on the** Pennsylvania Railroad are **supplied with injectors or rather** extinguishers, **does also show the great benefit of using an** injector **as a fire extinguisher.** The apparatus is placed underneath the foot plate of the locomotive **engine and it has** double discharge ends for hose **connections,** taking **the** supply water from the tender. **At a boiler** pressure of about 100 lbs. the extinguisher **is capable of** throwing out a double jet of water about 5-16 **of an inch in** diameter at a **very far distance and height, and it is intended to be** used for the extinguishing **of any** fire that will happen **to break out at any of** the Company's buildings, **as well as to render** assistance **to any** dwelling **house situated along-** side the Railroad **tracks.**

By the above, **we merely wish to call the engineers at-** tention to the fact, that an injector can be applied with advantages and **is of immense benefit in those localities,** where there are no other appliances for extinguishing fire on hand, or where the outside help is too far.

Such arrangements are often to be seen in large mills or factories situated in small country places.

———

On page 15, in the foot note, 1062 should be read 1202.